HOW TO WHISTLE SONGS

AN EASY, ENJOYABLE GUIDE TO BEAUTIFUL WHISTLING

BY

EDWIN ZILZ

TEACHER OF VOICE AND SPEECH

AUTHOR OF 'PRACTICAL GUIDE TO A BETTER SPEAKING VOICE'

THE STANTON PRESS
6715 HOLLYWOOD BOULEVARD
LOS ANGELES 28, CALIFORNIA

HOW TO WHISTLE SONGS

To

My Brother, Wilhelm Zilz, M.D.,
Whose Profound Scientific as well as Musical Knowledge
Has Been an Inspiration to Me.

TABLE OF CONTENTS

PREFACE

"HOW TO WHISTLE SONGS" is intended for everyone, old and young, who likes to whistle. Whistling not only enables you to express yourself musically but does so without requiring either an instrument or the use of the voice. Whistling enables you to create beautiful music whenever and wherever you wish. It brings you great and lasting enjoyment as well as the admiration of your family and friends. Furthermore, whistling with others in harmony offers an ideal opportunity for group activity.

Good whistling is characterized by pure, rich and mellow tones, produced with ease, on exact pitch and responsive to the thoughts and moods expressed in a song.

There is a definite need for practical instructions in the art of whistling, and I hope that my book will fill this need. Of course, one can whistle without proper technique, but there are much more satisfying results and they can be achieved much more quickly when this method is used.

If you follow these clear and simple instructions, you will not have the slightest difficulty and in a short time you will whistle so beautifully that you and all who hear you will be delighted. This applies to those who have not whistled before as well as to those who can whistle now, but are not pleased with the quality, the volume and the range of their whistling tones.

In order to present the subject in an easily understandable form, unnecessary details have been omitted and theoretical explanations have been reduced to a minimum.

"HOW TO WHISTLE SONGS" is concerned with melody whistling only, not with the imitation of bird calls.

Whether you play an instrument or not, you will find that this book also represents a fascinating way to add to your general musical knowledge and ability, and thereby to increase your enjoyment of all music.

The idea for this book was first conceived during my musical training with outstanding teachers in Germany, including studies in my native Dresden with Franz Compter, a pupil of the great Franz Liszt. It is the result of many years of research and experience as a teacher of voice and related subjects in the United States and in Germany.

Edwin Zilz

Los Angeles, California

BREATHING FOR WHISTLING

Good whistling depends, to a large degree, on the proper management of breath. The breath must be so managed that it can be used to best advantage in whistling.

Insufficient breath management spoils the tone quality, reduces the volume, may cause you to whistle off key, and makes sustaining of longer tones and whistling of longer phrases almost impossible. Moreover, when your breath control is inadequate, a breathy (H-like) sound precedes and/or accompanies your whistling, as if your exhaled breath were attempting 'to get in front' of the whistling tones.

Basically, breathing consists of respiratory movements which cause the chest cavity to expand and collapse alternately, thus taking air into the lungs and expelling it again. Normal, silent, life-sustaining breathing and breathing for whistling are not entirely identical processes. In normal, silent breathing, the inhalation and exhalation require approximately the same amount of time. In whistling, the inhalation period is comparatively short and the exhalation period is purposely prolonged. Breathing for whistling necessitates increased muscular activity to regulate the flow of exhaled air.

In the beginning, correct breathing for whistling must be done consciously and must be observed closely. After some practice, good management of breath will become automatic and you will follow the correct breathing technique without having to think about it. But remember, until it has become automatic, you must definitely think of your breathing while you whistle.

After some practice, good management of breath will become automatic and you will follow the correct breathing technique without having to think about it. But remember, until it has become automatic, you must definitely think of your breathing while you whistle.

The posture of your body has a considerable influence on your breathing. A proper posture allows for freer, smoother functioning of the organs and muscles involved in breathing for whistling.

The whole body should be in a natural, straight, but not strained, position. A feeling of ease and flexibility should be maintained. The upper part of the body neither leans forward nor sways backward. The muscles of the face, lower jaw, neck and shoulders are free from tenseness. The neck is not stretched. The head is neither dropped forward nor tilted backward to any noticeable degree. The shoulders are moved sparingly and are not raised.

When standing, the body rests mainly on the balls of the feet, not on the heels, with both feet firmly on the floor. The feet are placed sufficiently wide apart to establish a comfortable body balance. One foot is generally placed a few inches in front of the other. The weight of the body is either equally distributed, or the foot that is in front carries slightly more weight. The position of the feet may be changed occasionally but not too frequently.

When the posture of the body is incorrect, the breathing apparatus is likely to function improperly, resulting in inferior whistling tones.

Inhalation for whistling must be as effortless and noiseless as possible. You must neither be seen nor heard to breathe when you whistle. It should be noted here that it is not advisable to whistle during the inhalation. You whistle only while you exhale. Furthermore, no breath should escape through the nose or the mouth after the inhalation is completed and before you start to exhale for whistling. Inhale easily either through the nose or the mouth, or preferably, through the nose with the mouth slightly open, with the upper and lower teeth slightly apart.

A) During the Inhalation for Whistling:

First, the lower chest expands; that is, the lower ribs move slightly outward and upward. The diaphragm (the large muscle which separates the cavities of the chest and the abdomen) lowers and flattens, thus enlarging the chest cavity. Simultaneously, the abdomen expands; that is, the relaxed abdominal wall moves slightly outward and forward.

B) At the Start of and During the Exhalation for Whistling:

While the lower chest is still expanded, the lower abdominal wall is slightly but flexibly drawn in and up. The abdominal muscles contract, gradually and steadily pressing inward and upward in support of the expanded lower chest.

It is particularly this contraction of the abdominal muscles while exhaling that helps you to retain and to regulate your breath as needed for the support of whistling tones. (It should be understood that the abdominal muscles relax during the inhalation and contract during the exhalation for whistling.)

When exhaling for whistling, there is a state of balanced elastic tension in the muscles of the abdomen and lower chest, free from unnecessary tenseness or rigidity.

The steady and smooth flow of whistling tones depends largely on a slow emission of breath. While whistling, you exhale very slowly, allowing the expanded lower chest (the lower ribs) to sink in only very gradually. Try to retain the contraction of the abdominal muscles, while keeping the expanded lower chest from sinking in until nearly all the air has been exhaled and you are almost ready to take a new breath. There should be no sudden sinking in of the expanded lower chest or relaxing of the abdominal muscles, especially while you whistle the first or the second tone after the inhalation.

If you 'slump', that is, if the lower chest is not properly expanded and is too relaxed, or is permitted to sink in too soon after the inhalation, the breath will rush out too quickly. The resulting tones will be weak, unsteady or otherwise distorted and you will 'run out of breath' before the last tone or tones of your phrase are completed. However, too much pressure on the breathing muscles or exaggerated, forced 'pushing outward' of the lower chest or 'pushing in and upward' of the lower abdominal muscles during the exhalation should be avoided. This would result in whistling tones of inferior quality and may cause the tones to become sharp.

If you inhale too deeply, thereby taking too much breath all at once, too great a pressure will be exerted on the breathing apparatus, causing you to expel the breath too rapidly.

Remember, it is mainly during the initial period of

practice that you need to give special attention to the management of breath for whistling. It will soon become instinctive - an integral part of your whistling - and you will not be conscious of it any longer. If your thoughts were concentrated continually on the functions of the breathing apparatus while you whistle, your tones would lack spontaneity as well as proper tonal and emotional quality.

Exercises

The following physical and breathing exercises will help to improve the posture of the body and will develop strength and flexibility in the organs and muscles concerned in breathing for whistling.

Only a few of these exercises should be done at one time, gradually increasing the number of times an exercise is repeated. Any attempt to force physical development must be avoided. For instance, the exhalation should not be overly prolonged.

The exercises should be practiced without strain, tenseness or rigidity. Pause between exercises whether you are tired or not. See to it that practice is never carried to the point of physical exhaustion.

Usually, the exercises should be done in a standing position. However, it is also beneficial to practice them occasionally while sitting down. If possible and convenient, exercise in a room with an open window but without a draft. Collar and belt should be loosened.

Even though these exercises are perfectly harmless to the healthy individual, those with physical ailments should first consult a physician before practicing them.

Relaxing Exercises

Before you practice, try to relax mentally as well as physically for a few minutes. For this purpose, use the following exercise as a whole or in part:

1) A) Sit down. Close your eyes lightly. Relax the muscles of your entire body as much as possible.

B) Inhale and exhale fairly slowly, deeply and rhythmically.

C) Stand up and continue to inhale and exhale in this manner for a short while.

D) Rotate or revolve your head slowly with very little muscular effort, moving the head lightly from left to right, then from right to left.

E) Open and close your mouth several times with a sensation of ease in the muscles of the lips, tongue, soft palate, lower jaw, neck and shoulders.

F) Slowly bend your upper body forward, head downward. Return slowly to the erect standing position.

G) Lightly massage your face, lips, lower jaw and back of the neck.

This exercise, done as a whole or in part, especially the slow, fairly deep and rhythmic breathing, tends to relieve mental tension and tiredness which interfere with good whistling. Repeat this exercise several times in succession.

Another effective relaxing exercise is the following:

2)   Stand straight. At first consciously tense
       some of the muscles of your body, particu-
       larly those of the lower jaw, neck, shoulders,
       arms and legs. Then relax them as com-
       pletely as possible. Repeat several times in
       succession, primarily for the purpose of
       comparison between the physical sensations
       of tension and of relaxation. Repeat the
       same exercise also in a sitting position.

Physical Exercises

1) A) Slowly and evenly describe small circles with your shoulders; first the right, then the left, in the forward direction.

   B) First the right shoulder, then the left, in the backward direction.

   C) Both shoulders simultaneously, first forward, then backward. Avoid any strain or tenseness. Repeat several times.

2) A) Stretch your arms straight sideways to the level of the shoulders, parallel to the floor.

   B) Describe circles by swinging the arms rhythmically in the backward direction, palms down. Repeat.

3) A) Raise your arms straight upward and rise on your toes as high as you can without strain; abdomen in, chest out.

   B) Let your arms sink slowly to their normal, relaxed hanging position and let your heels touch the floor again. Do not tilt the head backward or stretch the neck. The muscles of the shoulders must be relaxed. Repeat.

4) A) Raise your arms straight upward.

   B) Stretch arms backward as far as you can without strain.

   C) Lower your arms again. Repeat.

5) A) Place your feet comfortably apart.

B) Stretch your arms straight upward.

C) Bend your trunk to the right side, then return to the upright position.

D) Bend your trunk to the left side, then return to the upright position.

E) Lower your arms again. Repeat.

6) A) Place your feet comfortably apart.

B) Clasp your hands behind your head.

C) With relaxed shoulders, swing the upper body slowly in circles, first three times in the left direction, then three times in the right direction. Inhale during the upward movement, exhale during the downward movement. Avoid undue strain. Repeat.

7) A) Place your feet comfortably apart.

B) Clasp your hands behind your head, elbows drawn backward. Keep your head erect.

C) Slowly bend the upper body forward without dropping your head.

D) Return slowly to the normal standing position. Avoid undue strain. Repeat.

Breathing Exercises

1) A) For noiseless inhalation place the tip of
       the tongue lightly on the edges of the
       lower front teeth. Inhale through the
       nose and mouth as if you were going to
       yawn, without actually yawning. Feel the
       cool air entering the nose and mouth
       cavities. Notice the comfortable open-
       ness and wideness of the throat cavity.
       The muscles of the lips, tongue, face,
       lower jaw and throat are relaxed. Exhale.
       Repeat several times.

    B) Inhale audibly (noisily). Exhale. Then
       inhale silently. Exhale. Alternate
       several times. Repeat.

2) A) Take a comfortable breath while the
       upper and lower lips and the upper and
       lower teeth are held slightly apart.
       After you have completed the inhalation,
       no breath should escape through the nose
       or mouth.

    B) Hold your breath for five seconds,
       mentally counting 1 - 2 - 3 - 4 - 5.

    C) Exhale through the nose and mouth
       simultaneously. Notice the sudden
       collapsing movement of the expanded
       lower chest. Repeat several times.

3) A) Inhale.

    B) Hold your breath for five seconds.

    C) Exhale as slowly as you can while pro-
       ducing a faint S, **TH** or **F** sound.

       Increase the period of exhalation grad-
       ually to ten, fifteen, twenty-five or more
       seconds.

       Repeat several times.

4) A) Inhale.

    B) Exhale, distinctly articulating the sound
       of **P** six times on one breath.

       Repeat, gradually increasing the number
       of **P** sounds produced on one breath.

5) A) Take three short breaths instead of
       taking one long breath.

    B) Hold your breath while mentally counting
       1 - 2 - 3.

    C) Exhale only a very small quantity of the
       breath supply.

    D) Again hold your breath while mentally
       counting 1 - 2 - 3.

    E) Exhale only a very small quantity of
       breath. Continue this until your breath
       supply is exhausted. Try to gradually
       increase the number of times you can do
       this exercise before your entire breath
       supply is exhausted.

6)   A) Inhale while mentally counting 1 - 2.

   B) Hold your breath while mentally counting 1 - 2.

   C) Exhale while mentally counting 1 - 2 - 3 - 4 - 5 - 6.

   Repeat, gradually increasing the number of counts for the exhalation without undue strain.

7)   A) Inhale while mentally counting 1 - 2 - 3.

   B) Hold the breath while mentally counting 1 - 2 - 3 - 4 - 5 - 6.

   C) Exhale while mentally counting 1 - 2 - 3 - 4 - 5 - 6.

   Keep the lower chest from sinking in and the abdominal muscles from relaxing too quickly during the exhalation.

   Repeat.

ATTACK OF WHISTLING TONES

In good whistling, the tones are produced softly but energetically, and first of all, beautifully. They are pure, rich and floating. The tones are produced with ease, not forced in the least. There is no evidence of direct effort in good whistling tones.

The start of a whistling tone is termed its attack. Proper attack and production of whistling tones depend primarily upon the smooth, coordinated functioning of the breathing mechanism, the mouth and the sense of hearing. Clearness of attack, as well as freedom from unpleasant tone qualities, are of fundamental significance. For example, a sort of clicking or grunting (K-like) sound immediately before the start of a whistling tone should be avoided.

While you whistle, you should have a comfortable feeling of very slight expansion within the mouth cavity. A similar sensation is experienced while yawning. Therefore, it is helpful to remind yourself occasionally of the physical sensation of a very slight yawn. (Of course, you only think of a yawn, you do not actually yawn while you whistle.) However, the back part of the mouth cavity should not enlarge too much by overly raising the soft palate (the back part of the roof of the mouth).

No breath should escape through the nose while you whistle. If part of your outgoing breath is allowed to pass through the nasal passages, the tones will assume an impure and breathy quality.

Resonation refers to the enrichment, the reinforcement or the amplification of tone by means of sympathetic vibration in the resonators. As a comparison, the strings of a violin alone are not sufficient to create good tones. It is the wooden structure of the violin itself that beautifies and amplifies the tones. In whistling, the tones are, to some extent, enriched in quality and enlarged in volume and carrying power as a result of their resonation in such resonators as the cavities of the mouth, nose and upper head. The whistling tones seem to 'float', filling the bony structure of your head with vibrations.

While whistling, you should not only expel the tones through the lips, but should also - mentally - direct or focus the tones to the roof of the mouth cavity and into the upper head cavity. You simply imagine that the tones, while they actually exit through the lips, are also projected to a focal area behind and above your eyes. You aim the whistling tones at this imaginary focal area. Such aiming or focusing is merely a mental impression, a matter of seeming rather than of reality, and is not in conformity with a strictly scientific point of view. Nevertheless, despite the absence of scientific confirmation, there are definite indications that this 'imaginary tone placement', if otherwise combined with proper whistling technique, aids in achieving a more beautiful whistling tone quality.

You must know what you want to hear. You must know how you want your tones to sound, not only while you are whistling, but before you start the tone. For the best possible attack, clearly anticipate the tone you wish to create; that is, picture the tone in your mind immediately before you whistle it. The tone, as well as its physical sensations within the mouth, must always be well fixed in your memory.

In passing from the first to the following tones of a phrase, be careful not to change the initial sensation of tone markedly. The initial sensation of the correctly produced whistling tone must not be lost, thus maintaining proper intensity and continuity of tone.

In summary, a good whistling tone is induced primarily by:

A) Your forming a clear, mental picture of the tone you want to whistle.

B) Proper management of breath.

C) Your desire to enrich the tone by directing it into an imaginary focal area while releasing it through the lips.

D) Flexibility of the lips, the tongue, the lower jaw and the soft palate, as outlined in detail elsewhere in this book.

E) Responsiveness of the organs and muscles involved in whistling to the thoughts and emotions expressed in the song.

HARMONIOUS OVERTONES IN WHISTLING

A good whistling tone consists of the fundamental tone and its harmonious overtones. The fundamental tone determines the pitch; the overtones sound in harmony with the fundamental tone and give the complete tone its distinctive quality. We hear the fundamental and its overtones blended as one tone. The effect is that of a single tone on a certain pitch with a light and delicate 'wave'.

The correctly produced, sustained whistling tone is actually a wavelike pulsation between two pitch levels, also called vibrato. The lower tone of this pulsation is the fundamental tone. It is on the exact pitch and is louder than the higher one. The continual return to this exact pitch is absolutely necessary. The lower tone of the vibrato pulsation appears to be somewhat darker and the higher one brighter in color. The sound of the fundamental and its overtones should be kept distinctly in mind. In whistling, these wavelike pulsations are produced by the quivering motions of the tongue. How the tongue produces these motions is described in detail in the chapter on the tongue.

Pitch extent and frequency are two basic elements of the vibrato. Pitch extent refers to the distance between the low and the high point of the vibrato pulsation within a complete tone. In other words, it refers to the amplitude or width of the vibrato movement. Frequency refers to the number of pulsations within a complete tone. In other words, it refers to the rate of speed or rapidity of the vibrato movement.

The most common pitch extent in a whistling tone is half a note (a semi-tone) from the fundamental. The pitch extent may also be a whole note, or it may be one and a half note, the third, the fourth, the fifth or, rarely, the octave above the fundamental tone. A vibrato with too wide a pitch extent should be avoided.

The vibrato pulsations must be even and regular, both in pitch extent and in frequency. Otherwise, the resulting complete tone will be off key. Sometimes a whistling tone is attacked on correct pitch, but as it is sustained, the tone becomes off key because of its uneven and irregular vibrato pulsations.

A sustained tone whistled without vibrato tends to be dull and lacking in vitality. Refined vibrato beautifies the complete tone. However, unduly conspicuous or exaggerated vibrato affects the quality of the complete tone unfavorably and tends to break up a sustained tone into fragments.

If the vibrato pulsations are too weak for the fundamental tone, the complete tone tends to be flat. If the vibrato pulsations are too strong for the fundamental tone, the complete tone tends to be sharp. Vibrato pulsations that are either too fast or too slow have an unpleasant effect on the complete tone and should be avoided. Naturally, a very soft tone must be whistled with only a very light vibrato. In 'pp' (the softest) the vibrato pulsations almost disappear. As soon as the loudness of tone increases, the vibrato again will become more pronounced.

When you whistle a sustained tone, start the tone without the vibrato. Then, very soon after the attack, add the vibrato pulsations to the complete tone.

Do not keep the vibrato pulsations going continually while you whistle. It is a matter of taste when and how frequently these vibrato pulsations should be used. The meaning of the song and the emotions you wish to express should somewhat influence your use of the vibrato.

COLORING OF WHISTLING TONES

Whistling tones have a definite 'color'. Imaginative use of tone color enables you to whistle more expressively.

Thinking of the sound of certain vowels while whistling aids considerably in achieving this tone color and in making the tones more beautiful.

For instance,

EE (as in deep)   is a high vowel in sound and color.

EY (as in late)   is a medium high vowel in sound and color.

AH (as in arm)   is a medium vowel in sound and color.

OH (as in more) is a medium low vowel in sound and color.

OO (as in mood) is a low vowel in sound and color.

You do not think of the letters and the spelling of these vowels, you think only of their actual sound quality or color.

The basic whistling sound most closely resembles the sound of the vowel EE. In good whistling, you combine or blend the basic sound color of the vowel EE with the sound color of OH. Purse your lips to whistle the basic sound and at the same time, think clearly of the sound of the vowel OH. While you whistle, keep this OH sound distinctly in mind, thus giving more color and expressiveness to the complete tone. The more clearly and distinctly you think of OH while you whistle, the fuller and rounder will be the complete whistling tone.

Every OH sound contains a certain amount of AH and OO sound quality. The AH quality contained in every OH refines and adds warmth to the complete whistling tone. The OO quality contained in every OH softens and darkens the complete whistling tone. In the tones of the middle range, the OH sound color is most evident. In lower tones and in descending phrases or passages, the OO sound color somewhat predominates; that is, you think slightly more of the darkening OO sound color. The lower you whistle, the clearer and more distinct should be the darkening OO color of the complete tone. Lower whistling tones have a darker color but should not be whistled too dark. Higher tones have a brighter color but should not be whistled shrill.

Some individuals tend to darken the very soft tones too much. Others have the wrong impression that a dark tone color increases the loudness of a whistling tone. This is an erroneous assumption. The dark tone color does not actually add more volume to the whistling tone. It may give you the impression of increased volume, but the tones sound louder and stronger only to you.

The EE sound color brightens the complete tone. In higher tones and ascending passages, the EE sound color somewhat predominates; that is, you think slightly more of the bright EE sound. The higher you whistle, the clearer and more distinct is the EE color. However, if the EE color of the higher tones becomes shrill, add more of the darkening OO color, so that the tone will become more beautiful and expressive. In other words, you 'mentally color' the basic EE sound with the darkening OO in order to eliminate any possible shrillness in tone quality. In practicing this, at first keep the color of the OO sound well in mind while you whistle. After some practice, think gradually less of the OO sound color until the tone becomes perfect.

Occasionally while practicing, think very clearly and distinctly of the sound color of EE. This will help to add brilliance to your whistling and to eliminate an excessive darkening in color of the low tones.

If the tones tend to have a more or less dull quality, it will help to have the color of the AH vowel sound clearly in mind while you whistle. Thus you 'mentally color' the complete tone with the softening and beautifying AH. After some practice, think gradually less of the AH sound color until the dullness of the tone disappears.

In general, make sure that the basic whistling sound and the thought of OH are blended into one tone.

THE LIPS

The flexibility and responsiveness of certain organs and muscles involved in whistling contribute materially to good tone production. These consist primarily of the lips and the tongue and to some extent, the lower jaw and the soft palate. On the other hand, their rigidity and immobility have an unfavorable effect, particularly on tonal clarity.

Beautiful, clear and steady tones can be whistled only when the lips, tongue, lower jaw and soft palate function properly. The right position, especially of the lips, is an absolute necessity. The improper pursing of the lips can instantly destroy a good whistling tone.

The center parts of the lips are brought as closely together as possible without actually touching each other. They are lightly pursed and drawn forward away from the front teeth. The center part of the pursed upper as well as lower lip must be kept from touching the front teeth and they must never touch each other. Otherwise, they would close, partly or completely, the small opening of the mouth, thus interfering directly with the free emission of exhaled breath and causing an unpleasant interruption in the flow of whistling tone.

There should be a certain amount of tension in the lips, particularly in the lower one, as well as in the corners of the mouth. However, the tension must be moderate. Any strain or rigidity must be prevented. Actually you move your lips very little while you whistle. But you should have a feeling of the center part of your pursed lower lip being gently drawn down and forward. At the same time you should have a feeling of the center part of your upper lip being drawn very gently upward. The downward and forward drawing of the pursed lower lip is felt definitely stronger than the upward drawing of the upper lip. The center part of the pursed lower lip is drawn slightly more forward than that of the upper lip.

The loudness of the whistling tones is increased not only by exhaling relatively more air, but also by slightly widening the small opening of the lips. When you whistle higher tones, you purse the lips more tightly and feel the tensing as well as the downward and forward drawing more distinctly in the center part of the lower lip. The higher the pitch of tone the smaller the opening of the lips. There is also slightly increased tension in the corners of the mouth. When you whistle lower tones, the lips are parted a little wider and are pursed somewhat more loosely. Also, the pursed upper lip is in a slightly more forward position than for higher tones.

In summary:

A) The Lower the Whistling Tones:

The greater the aperture of the lips;
The less the compression of the lips.

B) The Higher the Whistling Tones:

The smaller the aperture of the lips;
The greater the compression of the lips.

Generally, if the lower lip is too relaxed, the whistling tones tend to be flat. If the lower lip is tensed excessively, the tones tend to be sharp. Moreover, excessive tension in the lower lip can result in an unpleasant trembling of the lower jaw.

The lips are never turned inward or are they pursed too tightly. If the protrusion of the lips is overdone, the tones assume an impure quality. As mentioned earlier, it is very important that the pursed center parts of both lips do not touch each other while you whistle. Furthermore, the lips are held as quietly as possible. Unnecessary changes in the position of the lips are to be avoided, particularly while a sustained tone is whistled, as the slightest movement of the lips will affect the tone.

Your lips should be neither too dry nor too moist. Those individuals who habitually moisten their lips with the front part of their tongue should guard against doing this too frequently and too noticeably. An excessive quantity of saliva in the vicinity of the lips or in the front part of the mouth is likely to interfere with good whistling tone production. A sort of 'smacking of the lips' at the beginning of a phrase or passage must also be avoided. The teeth or dentures should be in the best possible condition.

Always remember distinctly the physical sensation of the properly pursed lips. Exercise your lips until they assume the proper position readily.

Exercises for the Lips

The following exercises are intended to develop flexibility and responsiveness of the lips. They should be practiced without whistling.

1) A) Put the lower lip over the upper lip and stretch.

    B) Put the upper lip over the lower lip and stretch.

    Avoid exaggeration. Repeat several times alternately.

2) A) Produce the sound of the consonant P (as in pool), very energetically and very slowly. Repeat several times in succession.

    B) Produce the sound of P very energetically and rapidly. Repeat.

    To produce the P sound correctly, the lips are lightly but firmly brought together. The lower lip should not touch the edges of the upper front teeth. The teeth are held slightly apart. A small amount of air pressure is built up behind the closed lips. Thus, for a moment, the flow of exhaled air is completely stopped in the closed mouth. Then the lips are suddenly and vigorously separated and the compressed air escapes in a somewhat exploding manner.

3)   Spread the lips wide, as if you were articulating the sound of EE (as in see). Then return the lips to their normal position and relax them. Repeat.

4)   Protrude the lips as if you were articulating the sound of OO (as in mood). Then return the lips to their normal position and relax them. Repeat.

5)   Spread the slightly separated lips sideways, as in a rather exaggerated grin. Then move the lips to a rounded and protruded shape, as for OO. Repeat. Start slowly, gradually increasing the rate of speed. Strive for flexibility of the lips.

6)   Move the protruded lips several times slowly in a circle. Relax the lips each time before repeating this exercise.

7)   Practice the following exercise with vigorous but elastic movements of the lips, and with as little audible vowel sound as possible; that is, without the full use of the voice for the vowel sounds:

Boo-Boo-Boo- Bee-Bee-Bee- Bee-Boo-Bee-

Boo- Mee-Moo-Mee-Moo- Fo-Pee-Fo-Pee-

Wee-Woo-Wee-Woo- White Wall-White Wall-

Pah-Pey-Pee-Poh-Poo   Fo-Po-Fo-Po-

Wasp-Whisp-Wasp-Whisp, etc.

Repeat several times in succession.

THE TONGUE

The tongue can move in various directions. It can draw back or stretch forward, groove, broaden, become thicker or thinner, etc. The front part of the tongue is capable of a greater variety of movements than its back part.

When you whistle, the tongue is in an elastic condition and is kept under limited control. There is, however, a very slight degree of tension in the tongue. The middle and back parts of the tongue are in a somewhat raised forward position in the mouth cavity, arched toward the roof of the mouth without touching it. There is a narrow space between the slightly elevated middle and back parts of the tongue and the roof of the mouth cavity, leaving only a relatively small channel through which the exhaled air passes to the lips.

Certain quivering motions of the tongue are essential to good whistling. These are delicate, rather rapid forward and backward, as well as upward and downward movements of the front and middle parts of the tongue. You produce these motions of the tongue from the following positions:

A) When whistling medium high or higher tones, place the tip of the tongue rather firmly but flexibly on the inside edges of the lower front teeth. Place the sides of the tongue gently on the inner surfaces and edges of the upper side teeth. The body of the tongue is broad.

B) When you whistle lower tones, hold the tip of the tongue flexibly on the lower inside of the lower front teeth around the region of their roots.

C) When you whistle very low tones, the tip of the tongue does not touch the teeth at all.

The middle and back part of the tongue is always fairly relaxed, lowered in position for lower tones and raised for higher tones.

The following example serves to demonstrate the rapid motions of the tongue which take place during whistling: Gently place the tip of the tongue on the inside edges of the lower front teeth and say softly, in rapid succession, 'You-You-You-You-You-You-You-You-You-You-You'. Use very little exhaled breath and vowel sound. Observe the quivering motions of the tongue.

Another example to demonstrate these quick motions of the tongue is to imagine that you hold a very small ball (the size of a pea) in your mouth, rolling on top of the front and middle part of your tongue. Now, in your imagination, let this part of your tongue bounce the little ball quickly and lightly up and down. The tip of the tongue remains stationary, touching the inside of the lower front teeth.

Such light and rapid quivering motions of the tongue are produced while you whistle, except for staccato tones or the whistling of very fast phrases and passages. To produce a pure, vibrating tonal effect and not an impure tremolo, these motions of the tongue should not only be light and rapid, but they should also be as even as possible.

If the quivering motions of the tongue are too strong or else uneven and irregular, your whistling tones will be unsteady and off key. When your tongue is rigid, these quivering motions of the tongue will be inadequate. Tenseness at the back of the tongue will also hinder the flexible motions of the more active front part of the tongue.

After a short period of practicing the following exercises, your tongue will become more elastic and the quivering motions can be produced easily and at will. They will become automatic and you will not have to concentrate on the position and the action of the tongue any longer when you whistle.

Exercises for the Tongue

By practicing these exercises, the tongue will develop the responsiveness, as well as the precision of movement, required for good whistling. The exercises should be practiced without whistling.

1) Alternately spread and point the tongue. In the spread position, the front part of the tongue rests on the lower lip of the opened mouth. In the pointed position, the tip of the tongue is slightly protruded. Repeat.

2) Protrude the tongue, pointing its tip down toward the chin, as far as you can without undue strain. Keep the tongue out for a moment, then draw it back into the mouth while the mouth remains slightly open. Keep the tongue in the mouth for a moment while the mouth remains slightly open. Repeat. Start slowly, very gradually increasing the rate of speed.

3) Protrude the tongue, pointing its tip up toward the nose as far as you can without undue strain. Then draw the tongue back again into the mouth. Repeat, gradually increasing the rate of speed.

4) Let the tongue rotate around your lips from right to left, then left to right. Repeat.

5) Open your mouth fairly wide. Move the tip of the tongue from the right corner of the mouth to the left corner, back and forth. Repeat.

6) Open your mouth fairly wide. Let the tip of the tongue touch the middle part of the upper lip, then the middle part of the lower lip. Repeat.

7) Combine Exercises 5 and 6. Practice them alternately.

8) Open your mouth. Let the relaxed tongue lie flat in the mouth. Then raise the tip of the tongue to the upper gum ridge and press the tongue against it. Lower the tongue again. Repeat.

9) Open your mouth. Let the tip of the tongue touch first the inside of the left cheek, then the inside of the right cheek. Repeat back and forth several times increasing the rate gradually.

10) Open the mouth slightly. Place the tip of the tongue on the inside surface of the lower teeth. Hold the tip of the tongue in this position and raise the sides of the tongue to touch the upper side teeth. Then lower the tongue again to its normal position. The lips and lower jaw are held quietly. Repeat.

11) Place the pointed tip of the tongue on the base of the inside of the lower front teeth (the gums). Then place the pointed tip of the tongue on the base of the inside of the upper front teeth. The lips and lower jaw are held quietly. Repeat.

12) Practice the following exercise rather rapidly with flexible tongue movements and with as little audible vowel sound as possible; that is,

without the full use of the voice for the vowel sounds:

To-Do-To-Do-To-Do-To-Do-To-Do-To-Do

So-Tho-So-Tho-So-Tho-So-Tho-So-Tho-So

Loo-Loo-Loo-Loo-Loo-Loo-Loo-Loo-Loo

Dlo-Dlo-Dlo-Dlo-Dlo-Dlo-Dlo-Dlo-Dlo-Dlo

Ldee-Ldee-Ldee-Ldee-Ldee-Ldee-Ldee

So-Lo-So-Lo-So-Lo-So-Lo-So-Lo-So-Lo

To-So-Lo-Do-To-So-Lo-Do-To-So-Lo-Do

No-No-No-No-No-No-No-No-No-No-No-No

T-D-T-D-T-D-T-D-T-D-T-D-T-D-T-D-T

K-T-K-T-K-T-K-T-K-T-K-T-K-T-K-T-K

THE LOWER JAW

The lower jaw is part of the structure forming the framework of the mouth. A flexible lower jaw allows for freer actions of the tongue and the lips. Therefore, the muscles of the lower jaw must function at all times without tenseness or rigidity.

When whistling, the lower jaw lowers. It should not move more than absolutely necessary. If the head is dropped too low, or if the lower jaw is pulled down, its muscles tighten.

Mental or emotional tension can also induce a tightening of the muscles of the lower jaw, thus preventing the elastic motions of the tongue and the lips.

Exercises for the Lower Jaw

The following exercises are designed to develop flexibility of the lower jaw for whistling:

1) Open and close your mouth several times in succession. Keep the lower jaw absolutely free from tenseness. No strength is applied. The lower jaw falls somewhat by its own weight. Repeat. Start slowly and gradually increase the rate of speed.

2) Stretch your mouth by yawning fairly deeply. Repeat this several times without tenseness.

3) Lower the relaxed lower jaw slowly as far as it can be done comfortably. Then raise the jaw again slowly and close the mouth. Repeat.

4) Swing the lower jaw gently from side to side while the mouth is slightly opened. Repeat, at first slowly, then more rapidly.

5) Move the lower jaw around in a rotary motion from right to left and from left to right. The muscles of the lower jaw and the neck should be as relaxed as possible. Repeat, varying the rate of speed.

6) Say softly and rather rapidly:

A) OO-OH-AH (As in mood-home-arm).

B) YAH-YAY-YEE-YOH-YOO (As in arm-late-deed-home-mood).

Repeat.

THE SOFT PALATE

The palate or roof of the mouth separates the mouth cavity from the nasal cavity. The front part of the palate (the area just behind the upper gum ridge) is the hard palate. It is rigid and immovable. The back part is the soft palate. It is movable. Its flexibility is also of significance in whistling.

In normal, silent breathing the soft palate is relaxed. In whistling, it elevates very slightly, thereby enlarging the mouth cavity somewhat, and at the same time closing the opening from the mouth cavity to the nasal cavity. That is, while you whistle, the soft palate elevates slightly from its normal, relaxed position, which helps to prevent the escape of exhaled air through the nasal passages.

When the soft palate fails to elevate, the fullness of the whistling tones will be reduced and the tones will assume a breathy quality, since part of the exhaled air will flow through the nasal passages. On the other hand, when the soft palate elevates too much, or if excessive tension exists in the muscles of the soft palate, the whistling tones will be impure in quality. Furthermore, you will experience uncomfortable pressure in the back part of the mouth.

Exercises for the Soft Palate

If you practice the given exercises, the soft palate will become more elastic and responsive, and will readily assume the desired position for good whistling.

1) Yawn. To induce a yawning sensation, the lips are held together very lightly, then the lower lip begins to sag. The upper and lower lips and the teeth separate. Distinctly feel the slight elevation of the soft palate and the slight expansion of the mouth cavity. The muscles of the face, lower jaw and the throat are relaxed. Repeat.

2) A) Yawn slightly and comfortably.

   B) Remember the physical sensation of a slight and comfortable yawn and try to reproduce it as well as you can without actually yawning. Observe the motions of the soft palate as it elevates slightly. Avoid tenseness or rigidity. Repeat.

3) Inhale. Hold the lips lightly together. Try to yawn without separating the lips. Feel the slight elevation of the soft palate and the slight expansion within the mouth cavity. Then yawn with the lips separated. Repeat.

4) Inhale. Yawn slightly. Exhale very slowly while voicing a rather sustained sigh. Notice the comfortable feeling of ease in the mouth cavity. Try to reproduce this sensation of very slight elevation of the soft palate and very slight expansion in the mouth cavity whenever you whistle. Repeat.

5)   A) Inhale. Yawn slightly. Feel the very slight elevation of the soft palate and the very slight expansion within the mouth cavity.

B) Think of the whistling sound without actually whistling.

C) Form the lips to produce the whistling sound without actually whistling.

D) Whistle a sustained sound, moderately loud, on a medium pitch and not too prolonged. Repeat.

6)   Say UNG-AH. Observe the lowering of the soft palate for the NG sound and the rising movement of the soft palate for the AH sound. Repeat.

7)   Say ING-ICK-ING-ICK-ING-ICK-ING-ICK. Observe the actions of the tongue as well as of the soft palate. Repeat.

Between practicing these exercises, lightly massa the areas of the lower jaw as well as the lips and the ba of the neck. Always strive for a state of ease.

PITCH, VOLUME AND RATE OF SPEED

Besides quality, a whistling tone has three other chief elements or major components: Pitch, Volume and Duration or Rate of Speed. Their appropriate blending is necessary to good whistling. Almost continuous changes and variations in the use of pitch, volume and rate of speed, in accordance with the markings of the song, are required for purposes of expressiveness, emphasis and contrast. They create greater variety of musical expression and bring out more fully the meaning and emotional content of a song.

PITCH

The pitch may be defined as the position or height of a tone - the degree of elevation of a tone on the musical scale. Everyone has a certain pitch range which is the distance between the highest and the lowest tone he can whistle. One of our objectives is to extend the limits of this range and to make fullest use of it. Care must be taken that changes from one pitch level to the next following one are executed in an easy manner and without loss of good tone quality.

Every note of a song should be whistled exactly on pitch without slurring or sliding up to it. Whistling the tone slightly too high means to sharpen it. Whistling a tone slightly too low means to flatten it. Such whistling off key (either sharp or flat) may be caused by:

A) Insufficient breath support (particularly when whistling very softly);

B) Excessive breath pressure in the lower chest and abdominal region during exhalation for whistling;

C) Irregular or uneven vibrato pulsations of the tone;

D) Whistling with too much volume (particularly the higher tones);

E) Inability to anticipate the desired pitch immediately before you whistle a tone;

F) Lack of concentration upon the exact pitch while whistling a tone;

G) Inability to hear yourself clearly and distinctly;

H) Mental and/or physical fatigue;

I) Mental and/or physical tension.

Unfavorable acoustical conditions may sometime cause the tone to flatten. A large, echoing room or hall may occasionally cause the tone to sharpen.

Some individuals have a tendency to whistle sustained tones flat. Some tend to flatten the end of a sustained tone or the end of a phrase or passage of a song. Some tend to flatten the tones of a very slow phrase or passage. Others tend to flatten the tones of compositions which are written in a minor key. When higher tones are whistled off key because they are too loud, the volume should not only be decreased immediately, but proper pitch and tone quality should be observed closely. Nervousness of the individual sometimes can result in whistling off key, particularly in sharpening higher tones. A too tense way of whistling may also induce sharpening. A too relaxed way of whistling may induce flattening.

When you whistle phrases and passages in an ascending direction, be sure that the tones are not sharpened. Conversely, when you whistle in a descending direction, be sure that the tones are not flattened. When you whistle scales, be careful to keep the second and third of the ascending major scale exactly on pitch. The same applies to the fourth and fifth of the minor scale. If you repeat two whistling tones at the interval of a major second (as in a trill), be sure you do not whistle the higher one of these two tones flat.

Think ahead - anticipate the desired pitch of the next following tone. Imagine the tone as clearly and distinctly as possible before you whistle it. If a tone is off key, correct it immediately by concentrating on the exact pitch.

The High Tones

The higher tones in whistling have a somewhat greater carrying power. The lower and middle tones have perhaps the greater power of expression. There is some similarity between the sound color of higher whistling tones and that of a violin.

The production of higher whistling tones requires slightly more breath support than that of lower tones. You support your breath somewhat more firmly when you whistle higher tones or ascending phrases and passages. Remember, for higher tones, your lips are more tightly pursed then for the lower ones. The tongue is broader and a little higher in the middle and back part of the mouth cavity. The higher tones should be particularly light, well-rounded and brilliant.

High tones should not be whistled with too much volume. When you whistle a tone, you should feel sure that you can whistle a few tones higher without impairing the quality. It is sometimes doubt in your ability to whistle high tones on pitch that makes their production rather difficult. When a group of tones, a phrase or passage runs from the middle or the low range into the upper range, the lower tones are whistled with a little less than medium loudness. This tends to prevent the forcing of the high tones and allows for a smoother delivery. Whistle very gently from lower or middle tones to high tones. Furthermore, high tones should not be unduly prolonged just for reasons of musical effect.

The Low Tones

To produce lower whistling tones, your lips are somewhat less tightly pursed than for higher tones. The middle and back parts of the tongue are lowered slightly. The front part of the tongue is slightly retracted. The low tones must also be well-rounded and clear, not too dark in color.

When a group of tones, a phrase or passage runs

from higher or middle tones into the low range, the higher and middle tones should be whistled with a little less than medium loudness. This can prevent the weakening of low tones and will allow for a smoother delivery. Whistle very lightly from higher and middle tones into the low range.

VOLUME

Volume in whistling refers to the degree of loudness, the quantity of tone. Good whistling requires adequate volume as well as variations in volume of tone, consistent with the musical score and the meaning and emotional content of the song.

The physical actions that cause either the increase or the decrease of tone volume are mentally induced. Specifically, when you want to increase the volume, you think the tone louder; that is, you will the tone volume to increase. This causes the following to occur:

Inhalation

A) A relatively larger quantity of air is inhaled.

B) The lower chest (the lower ribs) and the relaxed abdominal wall move slightly more outward.

Exhalation

C) Then, during the exhalation and whistling, the lower abdominal muscles contract somewhat more firmly. They are drawn more decidedly but still very flexibly inward and upward in support of the expanded lower chest.

D) A relatively larger quantity of air is exhaled.

E) The pursed lips are slightly more tensed.

The louder you whistle, the firmer should be the support of breath in the expanded lower chest and particularly in the abdominal muscles. However, there should be no uncomfortable tenseness either in the muscles of the lower chest and the abdomen or in the lips, tongue, soft palate, lower jaw or neck as a result of an increase in tone volume. Also, there should be no material change in quality and steadiness of tone whether the tone volume is increased or decreased.

Increase in volume is called crescendo. Decrease is called decrescendo or diminuendo. You can whistle crescendo or decrescendo one or more times on a sustained tone, or the crescendo and decrescendo may also be extended over a phrase, a passage, a trill, etc.

Usually, a sustained whistling tone should have a crescendo, or decrescendo, or both. In many instances, a sustained tone is attacked very softly and then the volume is increased evenly and gradually until it has reached a medium or above medium degree of loudness. This is sustained very shortly. Then the tone is evenly ended as softly as it was started. The increase and decrease of tone volume must be at a rather steady pace, not too abrupt or too rapid, and in accordance with the time value and character of the respective notes.

The beginning of a sustained tone or the beginning of a phrase should not be accented habitually. On the other hand, the beginning of a sustained tone or the beginning of a phrase should not be whistled too hesitantly or weaken immediately following the attack.

Be sure that ascending phrases or passages are not whistled crescendo habitually. On the other hand, be sure that descending phrases or passages are not whistled decrescendo habitually.

The increase in whistling tone volume requires a little more breath than the decrease. The tone sometimes tends to rise slightly in pitch during the increase in volume and tends to fall slightly in pitch during the decrease in volume. Therefore, in the beginning you may have a tendency to whistle the crescendo sharp and to whistle the decrescendo, particularly the end of a decrescendo, flat. There is also a tendency toward an unsteadiness of tone when whistling decrescendo. This should be avoided.

You should always whistle with sufficient volume of tone so that you can be heard without effort. Avoid lowering or raising the head to a considerable degree in an effort to project your whistling tones. When whistling in a large room or hall, you should not only whistle somewhat louder than usual, but sometimes also at a relatively slower rate of speed. There is a psychological element in whistling tone projection, as well as a physical one. You should have a definite desire to project your tones to the opposite wall.

The degree of tone volume should also be adapted to the acoustical conditions of the room or hall. The ceiling, the walls and the floor, as well as the furnishings of the room or hall in which you whistle, have an influence on the carrying power of your tones. For example, hard plaster is considered to be a preferred material because it permits greater reflection of tone. Such materials as heavy curtains or draperies, heavy rugs or carpets absorb more of the sound and permit less reflection. It is equally unfavorable to whistle in a room or hall while facing one or more open windows or open doors. Try out your whistling tones in rooms and halls of various sizes and conditions, using varying degrees of tone volume.

In the beginning of your whistling practice, do not increase the tone volume considerably, at least not until you can produce the very soft and the medium loud tones easily and satisfactorily.

The most frequent faults to be avoided in relation to the use of volume in whistling are:

A) A too weak tone;

B) A too loud tone;

C) Lack of or insufficient variety in tone volume;

D) Exaggeration in the variation of tone volume.

RATE OF SPEED

The rate of speed, pace or tempo in whistling refers to two basic elements:

1) The duration or prolongation of the tones - the length of time each tone is sustained.

2) The length of pauses between tones, between phrases and between passages.

A phrase may be described as one unit of a musical composition - a portion of a theme or melody. A passage consists of two or more successive phrases.

One of the fundamental requirements of good whistling is to give each note its full time value in accordance with the musical score and to maintain the proper tempo, also in accordance with the meaning and emotional content of the song.

A bright, brilliant tone color is used in fast whistling. Rapid phrases and passages should be whistled with an especially 'happy' feeling. You will notice that rapid phrases and passages can be whistled better when the tone volume is rather moderate. Whistling too rapidly should be avoided. It tends to induce a tightening of the lips, the lower jaw and associated muscles. This invariably results in interference with good whistling tone production. Abrupt changes in the rate of speed should also be avoided.

The rate of speed is not necessarily or habitually slowed down:

A) When whistling very softly;

B) When whistling a decrescendo;

C) When whistling a descending phrase or passage.

The rate is not necessarily or habitually accelerated:

A) When whistling relatively loud;

B) When whistling a crescendo;

C) When whistling an ascending phrase or passage.

For instance, occasionally it is very impressive to whistle an ascending passage with increasing tone volume and a slowing of the rate.

Legato whistling refers to a continuous, sustained and unbroken series of tones. Legato tones are whistled in smooth succession. They are sustained firmly and are connected from one tone to the next following one. Special attention should be paid to the exact pitch of each legato tone. Proper legato whistling requires particularly good management of breath. Indeed, it is impossible to whistle good legato tones when your breath support is insufficient. Gliding from one tone to another should be done without any unnecessary break or careless slide. In written music, legato is expressed by a curved line over two or more notes.

The opposite of legato is staccato. Staccato whistling refers to one or more tonal attacks in rapid succession. Each tone is cut short and disconnected from the next one. Staccato tones should be whistled softly, as crystal-clear as possible. Staccato tones require somewhat less breath, but also very good management of breath. It is a matter of goo taste not to whistle staccato tones too penetratingly. Furthe more, they should not be whistled too hurriedly. Never 'lose a single staccato tone or whistle staccato tones carelessly. Staccato tones, just as the rapid phrases and passages, are whistled in a rather vivacious and light manner.

As soon as you can whistle staccato tones well, your sustained tones are more likely to be satisfactory, too. For developing flexibility, as well as for the gradual extension of the pitch range, staccato exercises are helpful. They are also of particular use in developing the very soft (pp) tones, and in improving or eliminating breathy whistling tone quality. In written music, staccato is expressed by a small round dot over each note.

Rests do not serve merely for inhalation purposes. Specific symbols in the musical score indicate the length of the silence equal in length to the notes which they replace. Every rest, as indicated in the score, should receive full consideration. Do not whistle through rests. They are as essential a part of the song as the notes.

The rate may, to some extent, be adapted to the size of the room or hall and its acoustical conditions. It is some times advisable to whistle a song, or part of it, somewhat slower in a large room or hall.

The most frequent faults to be avoided in relation to the use of rate of speed in whistling are:

A) Too slow rate;

B) Too fast rate;

C) Lack of or insufficient variety in rate of speed;

D) Exaggeration in the variation of rate of speed;

E) Pauses between phrases and between passages of the song that are too long or too short.

EXPRESSION OF EMOTIONAL QUALITIES
IN WHISTLING

Your imagination plays an important part in good whistling. Whistling, like any other form of musical art, demands emotional expression combined with technique. In whistling, good results are not achieved in a purely mechanical manner. You cannot create beautiful whistling tone by physical action and applied knowledge alone. Whistling is also the result of your thinking and feeling.

If you do not put 'heart' into your whistling tones, they will have an empty quality, no matter how perfect your technique may be. The more responsive you are to various moods and emotions, the easier it will be for you to reflect them in your whistling tones. The appropriate emotional quality appears in the tones when you concentrate on the meaning of the song and when you really feel what you want to express.

Enter the mood of a song or of a certain phrase or passage, not only while you whistle it, but at least one bar before you start. Then try to sustain this mood as long as required by the meaning of the song. Every tone, every phrase and passage must be whistled with spirit, sincerity and enthusiasm.

Some of the different moods or emotional reaction that can be expressed in whistling are joy, excitement, courage, humor, determination, tenderness, seriousness, reverence, calmness, sadness, etc.

An emotionally unresponsive or an indifferent person is more likely to produce colorless, inexpressive whistling tones.

Good whistling affects the emotions as well as the ear of the listener. When you thoroughly enjoy whistling a song, chances are the listener will enjoy it too. There is something thrilling about the silvery sound of whistling a melody, something that seems to touch everyone with happiness. It gives you a thrill to let your whistling tones 'rise' above the musical accompaniment of an instrument, an orchestra or a recording.

PRACTICE OF WHISTLING EXERCISES

The following exercises are designed to develop the quality, the volume and the flexibility of your whistling tones and to extend the pitch range. Understand the purpose of an exercise and practice it carefully. Practice the exercises with varied volume of tone and rate of speed, but always with clarity and ease. Proper execution of an exercise is more important than the quantity of exercises. Two or three exercises practiced thoughtfully are more effective than many exercises practiced rather carelessly. It is not as important how much you practice for whistling but how you practice.

The exercises consist mainly of fragments of scales, of arpeggios (whistling of the notes of a chord in rapid succession) and of little technical figures.

The exercises given here are written in the key of 'C' and should, of course, be transposed as you go up and down the scale, as low or as high as your range will allow you to whistle. Start most exercises in the middle of your range and from there go first down the scale, then return to the middle range. Then go up the scale and return to the middle range. Progress by a half-note (a semi-tone) for each repetition. The tones of the middle range must be developed first before going very low or very high.

In all exercises, the loudest, the lowest and the

highest tones must not be practiced too much. Most attention should always be given to good tone quality, and you should not try to whistle louder, lower or higher than you can do comfortably. In extending the pitch range, no forcing is necessary. Practice of the given exercises should enable you to develop greater volume of tone, a wider pitch range, as well as better quality of tone. Whistle softly from an easy middle range into the upper range. The high tones, at first, are lightly touched but not sustained. Gradually, they may be sustained. Never 'hit' or force the high tones; instead whistle them softly and beautifully.

It should be noted that the exercises are to be practiced with animation rather than making them a more or less dull and uninspiring succession of whistling tones. When you repeat an exercise two or more times, maintain the same spontaneity and buoyancy for each repetition, consistently striving for beauty and purity of tone.

Think of the exercise while you inhale. As explained repeatedly, anticipate each tone (its quality, pitch, volume and duration) immediately before you whistle it. Remember the physical sensation that produces the whistling tone. While you whistle, experience simultaneously a dual sense of hearing your tone and of physically feeling the actions that produce it.

Pause between exercises, relaxing mentally as well as physically before you continue to practice.

At first it is not advisable to practice by whistling entire songs. Practice the given exercises only. Then, practice some of the melodic passages from your favorite songs and, finally, practice complete songs.

Try to induce a calm, tension-free state of mind. Gently massage the relaxed muscles of the face, lips, lower jaw and back of the neck before you start to practice.

Occasionally, use a mirror for practice purposes to observe your facial expressions while you whistle.

Exercises #15, 16, 17, 18, 19, 20:

Whistle a gradual and even crescendo, decrescendo, or both, on one or more notes, as indicated. When increasing the tone volume, no forcing is required. When decreasing the volume, a possible flattening of tone should be avoided. Repeat.

Exercises #3, 4, 8, 24:

Repeat each of these exercises four times in succession. Start very softly, each time slightly increasing the tone volume. Repeat.

Exercises #1, 7, 11:

Stand approximately three feet in front of a wall, facing it. Repeat these exercises several times. Then step back two feet and repeat the same slightly louder. Then step back two feet and repeat the exercises again slightly louder. Repeat this procedure several times.

Exercises #2, 5, 6, 30:

The legato, as indicated, should be well observed. Glide smoothly from one tone to the next following one. Repeat.

Exercises #9, 13, 14, 29:

The staccato, as indicated, should be well observed. Whistle every tone clearly and distinctly, exactly on pitch. Do not connect one tone with the next following one. Repeat.

Exercises #10, 12, 31:

Some of these exercises combine legato and staccato and should be carefully executed. Repeat.

The following exercises contain grace notes, ornaments or embellishments which add to the attractiveness of the song you whistle. Most frequently used are the appoggiatora or leaning note, the trill, the turn and the mordent.

Exercise #32: (Appoggiatora or Leaning Note)

The appoggiatora is a short note, whistled in a very light and crisp manner, either before or following the principal note. The principal note is slightly accented. Repeat.

Exercises #21, 22, 23: (Trill)

The trill is a rapid alternation of the given note and the next higher note. The trill may also begin with the higher note and end on the lower one. The upper note is slightly accented. Attack the trill purely in quality and exactly on pitch. Keep the rhythm regular. Repeat.

Exercise #25: (Turn)

The turn is composed of the note immediately above the principal note, the principal note, the note immediately below the principal note, and again the principal note. Repeat.

Exercise #26: (Inverted Turn)

The inverted turn is composed of the note immediately below the principal note, the principal note, the note immediately above the principal note, and again the principal note. Repeat.

Exercise #27: (Upper Mordent)

The upper mordent is a very rapid alternation of the principal note, the note immediately above the principal note, and again the principal note. The first two notes are very short; the last one is slightly accented. Repeat.

Exercise #28: (Lower Mordent)

The lower mordent is a very rapid alternation of the principal note, the note immediately below the principal note, and again the principal note. The first two notes are very short; the last one is slightly accented. Repeat.

Exercises #29, 30, 31: (Triplets)

The first note of each group of three receives a very slight rhythmic accentuation. Whistle each triplet with clear distinction. Repeat.

The study of music theory is not within the scope of this book. Those who wish to increase their knowledge of this subject will find several good books available.

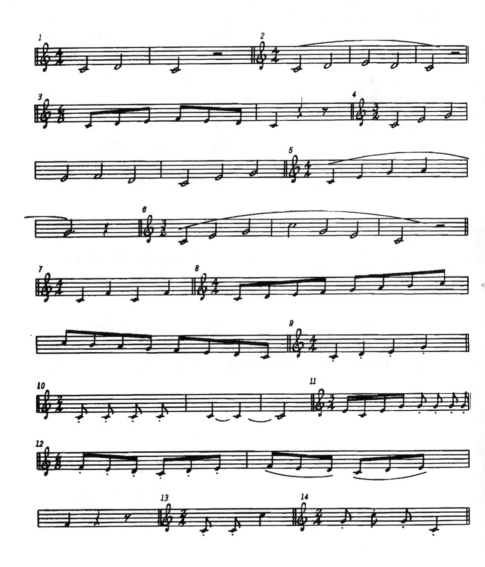

WHISTLING OF SONGS

When you whistle a song, you should concentrate mainly upon the music, the melody, not upon whistling technique. You are ready to whistle songs when the mechanical (physical) phases of whistling have become so automatic that you have to pay little attention to them.

If you want to phrase properly while whistling a song, you must be well supplied with breath at all times. The entire delivery of a song depends to a large extent on slow, controlled exhalation. The longer the phrase, the better must be the breath support.

Always preserve a sense of continuity in the melody This continuity within a song should not be interrupted unnecessarily. If you take too much time to inhale, the rhythm and the melodic unity of the song are likely to suffer. Renew your breath without any obvious stoppage, without unduly interrupting logically connected tones, the rhythm or the melody of a song. If necessary, try to shorten very slightly the last note before taking a new breath. In this way, you will have a little more time to inhale, and still whistle the first tone after the inhalation accurately on time.

Measure the coming phrase quickly in your mind before as well as while you whistle it. Hold the phrase in mind as a unit, not as a series of individual tones. Thus, you will regulate instinctively the quantity of air used in accordance with the character and length of the phrase. You will arrange to have your breath supply last until you can logically pause for a moment to inhale without unduly interrupting or disturbing the melody line.

When a phrase is too long to be whistled in one breath, the beginning tone after renewing your breath should be whistled with much the same quality and volume as the tone that was whistled immediately before you stopped for breath.

You should always be able to whistle a few more tones at the moment you are about to take a new breath. It is important to inhale before you are conscious of being completely out of breath.

Exactness in the whistling of the first and the last tone of a phrase must be assured. Whistle the first tone of a phrase especially well. Then think and hear this same good tone quality while gliding to the second and the next following tones of the phrase. Retain the initial physical sensation.

When you pass from the first tone to the second and the following tones, change the position of the lips as little as possible. Moreover, do not close your lips completely just before or while renewing your breath.

Keeping proper time is one of the main factors of whistling a song effectively. Every note and every rest must be given its time value. Do not lengthen notes unduly, and do not pause longer or more often than required. Observe the key and changes in key as well as the various distinctions in the loudness and in the rate of speed of a song. If you have a copy of the song you intend to whistle, prepare yourself by marking it in advance as to where and when you want to inhale, where you want to pause, where you want to increase and decrease the volume as well as the rate of speed. Become thoroughly familiar with the song.

Classical compositions should be whistled as they were written. In lighter songs, when you wish to make certain changes, adhere to these changes and do not make new changes every time you whistle the song. Sometimes you may want to whistle one or more sustained notes while the accompanying music plays a different group of notes. Occasionally you may want to whistle, for example, the sustained note one fifth higher than the key note. Or you may want to whistle a melodious group of notes while the accompaniment plays one or more sustained notes. It is up to you, your musical taste and judgment to decide this in each case.

Nervousness prevents the mind, the organs and muscles concerned in whistling from functioning well. When you are nervous or excited while whistling a song, more oxygen is used, more breath is wasted and more frequent inhalations are required. If you whistle in the presence of listeners, do not think of them while you whistle. Think of what you whistle and how you want to whistle it.

The sound of one or more musical instruments can easily prevent you from hearing your own tones distinctly. Therefore, when you whistle with instrumental accompaniment (or perhaps using recorded music for accompaniment), do not stand too close to an instrument or the record player. The tones of the melody predominate and are normally stronger than those of the accompaniment. The accompaniment must be subordinated to the whistling tones, unless the whistling itself supplies the accompaniment, as sometimes may be the case.

Listening to music whenever and wherever possible will help you to develop your appreciation of it, as well as your interpretative ability in whistling.

GROUP OR CHORAL WHISTLING

Any number of people (even as few as two or three) can whistle together in harmony as a group or 'choir'. For instance, three part harmony sounds very beautiful in whistling. The fundamental requirements for the harmonious blending of these parts in group whistling are practically identical to those in choral singing. Thus, many musical selections composed for choir can be adopted easily for whistling.

Whistling offers an ideal opportunity for group activity. It is an excellent medium of group musical expression for adults and youngsters alike. This simple form of group music making provides a source of relaxation and pleasure, and enables each participant to share his musical enjoyment with others. Group whistling of songs may be enjoyed, for example, in the home, in recreation or assembly halls, on the hiking trail, around the fireplace or the campfire, etc.

All technical instructions given previously in this book are also applicable to group whistling. Every participant should study the book and know how to whistle in order to perform well in a group.

As mentioned, a most beautiful effect in group whistling is achieved with three-part harmony. For purposes of identification, the three parts or divisions will be called soprano, mezzo-soprano and alto. Of course, men as well as women whistle within the range of these three parts.

Since the soprano part carries most of the melody of the song, the appropriate ratio would be: Three sopranos, one mezzo-soprano and one alto. This same ratio can be doubled, tripled, etc. The whistling of the harmony-creating mezzo-soprano and alto parts is just as important as the whistling of the soprano part.

Each participant should be able to whistle within a tonal range of one and a half to two octaves.

The lowest note of the soprano whistling range is approximately 'B' below middle 'C'.

The lowest note of the mezzo-soprano whistling range is approximately 'F' below middle 'C'.

The lowest note of the alto whistling range is approximately 'C' below middle 'C'.

Those whistling the soprano parts are placed to the left, the mezzos in the middle, the altos on the right side, fairly close together, in a semi-circle and directly in front of the leader.

The leader of a whistling choir does not need to be an accomplished musician or choral director. The leader should, however, be thoroughly familiar with the whistling techniques outlined in this book and be able to whistle along with the group. His major requirements, in addition to that, are a good ear, some knowledge of music, a pleasant personality, patience and sufficient enthusiasm. The leader's enthusiasm will be 'infectious' and the group will reflect it.

Each participant should be made to feel that group whistling is a pleasure - fun rather than a task. Moreover, the rehearsal should give each member of the group a sense of accomplishment.

A friendly and cheerful leader will usually have the attention and cooperation of the group. He must assume an encouraging rather than an overly critical atti tude. But he should be firm as well as kind.

Rehearsals should always take place in an orderly manner. Too frequent and/or prolonged practice sessions are to be avoided. The leader plans every practice or re hearsal session in advance. He familiarizes himself with th song or songs he intends to rehearse with the group. A variety of songs is of particular importance, lighter songs alternating with more serious selections. The leader pre- pares a list of suitable songs. This list may be enlarged gradually and the participants asked to suggest some of thei favorite songs to be included.

If he feels the necessity to increase his knowledge, the leader will find excellent books on choir directing.

At the beginning of each group rehearsal, a few minutes may be devoted to practicing some of the breathing and whistling exercises. This will result in increased re- sponsiveness and efficiency of each participant. In addition the following four exercises will be helpful in preparing a group, especially an inexperienced one, for whistling in harmony:

1)   A) The leader whistles and sustains a tone
         for several beats while the entire group
         listens.

     B) Then every member, one by one, whistles
         the same tone.

     C) This procedure is repeated at various
         pitch levels.

2)   A) The leader sustains a tone for several
         beats while the entire group listens.

     B) Then, the members of one division only
         (either soprano, mezzo or alto) repeat
         the same tone.

     C) This procedure is then repeated with
         another sustained tone for each of the
         other divisions.

     D) Finally, all divisions whistle their re-
         spective sustained tone simultaneously
         and in harmony.

     E) This procedure is repeated at different
         pitch levels.

3)   A) The entire group whistles a passage
         from a song (the melody or soprano
         part) several times very softly while
         the leader whistles the mezzo part.

     B) The same is repeated with the leader
         whistling the alto part.

4)   The accompanist plays a passage from a
     song (the melody or soprano part). At the
     same time:

     A) The leader and the entire group whistle
         the mezzo part of the song.

     B) The leader and the entire group whistle
         the alto part of the song.

     C) The mezzo and the alto divisions both
         whistle in harmony with the accompanist's
         melody or soprano part of the song.

When a song is rehearsed:

A) At first the entire group whistles the song
    several times in unison from beginning to end.
    Everybody whistles the melody or soprano part.

B) Then, one division at a time rehearses its own
    part only (soprano, mezzo-soprano and alto).

C) Finally, all divisions are combined and the
    entire group whistles the song together in har-
    mony.

While one division rehearses its part, the other
divisions must always listen quietly and attentively. Group
whistling requires that each participant listen closely not
only to his part but also to the other part or parts, striving
to make his part blend or harmonize with the others. The
leader must be particularly sensitive to balance of tone
and must merge all parts into a harmonious blend.

When rehearsing, the more difficult or the higher
phrases or passages of a song may, at first, be practiced
separately, perhaps at a slower rate of speed or on an

easier pitch level. After some practice, the entire song should be whistled as composed.

Some sections of certain songs may be whistled in unison rather than in harmony. Songs whistled in unison, or songs having relatively many unison phrases or passages, require less rehearsal time than songs whistled in harmony.

Many songs lend themselves to be whistled with solo parts, duets, trios, etc. More or less short solos may be included to make group whistling of familiar songs more stimulating. Different members of the group should be chosen to whistle these solos, duets, etc.

The easier and the more difficult songs are to be practiced alternately. This tends to hold and to increase interest and has a refreshing effect on the group. Song books may be made available to the participants. Whenever possible, a song should be memorized.

The simultaneous, precise attack of tone of all participants as well as the precision in the ending of the last tone of a phrase or passage are essential requisites to the blending in group whistling. The attack and the ending of a phrase or passage must be definite as well as simultaneous, in accordance with the musical score. Furthermore, all participants must glide from one tone to the next following tone at the same instant. Therefore, every participant watches the leader who must be clearly visible to the entire group. The leader cannot give the signal for the start of a song until he has the attention of the entire group.

The leader, as well as the group, should be familiar with the simple patterns of conducting 2/4, 3/4, 4/4 and 6/8 time. He has various ways to relay his instructions or intentions. For example, he may indicate increases in tone volume by stronger hand and arm movements. He may indicate decreases in tone volume by gradually drawing the fingertips of his hand toward the thumb, or by gradually and slowly moving his hand toward the mouth. Increases in tone volume may also be indicated by letting the palm of the hand face upward. Conversely, decreases in tone volume may be indicated by the palm facing downward.

If a tone is sustained, the left hand may be raised while the tone is whistled. Very shortly before the end of a composition, before the flow of tone stops, one or both hands may be raised several inches as a preliminary sign; then the hand or hands lowered again, more or less decisively, to indicate the actual ending. The end of a sustained tone usually calls for a light and rapid downward motion of the left hand. A stop may also be signalled by the raised hand, with the palm facing forward and outward. Staccatos may be indicated by short, distinct beats from the wrist. In any case, excessive gestures should be avoided. From time to time the leader may also indicate changes by his own whistling along with the group.

Group whistling is very effective, either with or without musical accompaniment. The accompaniment should always be played softly - subordinated. The accompanist or accompanists must be able to see the leader clearly. When unaccompanied, a pitch pipe may be used for the entire group; or perhaps one pitch pipe for each division, one specific member of each division using a pitch pipe.

If one of the participants whistles off key habitually, the exactness of pitch of the entire group may be unfavorably affected. Those participants who always sharpen or flatten should not be included in the group.

If available, a phonograph record of the rehearsed song (either instrumental or vocal) should be played and repeated. The occasional use of a tape recorder for practice or rehearsal purposes is also helpful.

A LIST OF SONGS TO WHISTLE

There is an almost unlimited number of musica
compositions that can be whistled beautifully. This include.
besides the classical and semi-classical compositions, mai
of the currently popular songs as well as the old favorites.
Some of them are listed here.

Religious songs, Christmas songs, folk songs and
children's songs are also delightful to whistle. Many opera
and light operas have especially melodious parts, arias an
songs suitable for whistling. If you like, you can also
whistle certain parts of symphonies and concertos, as we
as numerous selections originally composed for voice or
for musical instruments.

Here are the titles of some of the best-loved songs
which are very suitable for whistling:

"Abide With Me" - Monk

"Adeste Fidelis" - Reading

"Ah! Sweet Mystery of Life" (Naughty Marietta) - Herbert

"All the Things You Are" (Very Warm for May) - Kern

"All Through the Night" - Owen

"America the Beautiful" - Ward

"Andante Cantabile" - Tchaikowsky

"Ave Maria" - Schubert

"Ave Maria" - Bach-Gounod

"Barcarole" (Tales of Hoffmann) - Offenbach

"Battle Hymn of the Republic" (Civil War Song)

"Beautiful Dreamer" - Foster

"Because" - D'Hardelot

"Begin the Beguine" (Jubilee) - Porter

"Believe Me, if All Those Endearing Young Charms" - Irish
    Air

"Beyond the Blue Horizon" (Monte Carlo) - Whiting

"Blue Danube" (Waltz) - Johann Strauss, Jr.

"By the Waters of Minnetonka" - Lieurance

"Carry Me Back to Old Virginny" - Bland

"Children's Prayer" (Hænsel and Gretel) - Humperdinck

"Claire de Lune" - Debussy

"Come Where My Love Lies Dreaming" - Foster

"Cradle Song" - Schubert

"Dancing in the Dark" (Band Wagon) - Dietz-Schwartz

"Dark Eyes" - Mastren

"Dearly Beloved" (You Were Never Lovelier) - Kern

"Deep in My Heart" (Student Prince) - Romberg

"Deep River" (Traditional) - Arr. by Burleigh

"Drink to me Only" (Old English Air) - Jonson

"Embraceable You" (Girl Crazy) - Gershwin

"Elegie" - Massenet

"Emperor Waltz" - Johann Strauss

"Evening Star Song" (Tannhaeuser) - Wagner

"Falling in Love With Love" (Boys from Syracuse) - Rodgers and Hart

"First Noel" (Traditional)

"Flower Waltz" (Nutcracker Suite) - Tchaikowsky

"From the Land of the Sky Blue Water" - Eberhart-Cadman

"Going Home" (Largo, New World Symphony) - Dvorak

"Gold and Silver Waltz" - Lehar

"Hills of Home" - Calhoun-Fox

"Home Sweet Home" - Bishop

"Hymn to the Sun" (Le Coq D'Or) - Rimsky-Korsakoff

"I'll Follow my Secret Heart" (Conversation Piece) - Coward

"I Love You" - Grieg

"I Love You Truly" - Bond

"I'm Always Chasing Rainbows" (Dolly Sisters) - McCarthy-Carroll

"I'm Falling in Love With Someone" (Naughty Marietta) - Herbert

"In the Still of the Night" - Porter

"It's A Lovely Day Tomorrow" (Louisiana Purchase) - Berlin

"I've Got You Under my Skin" (Born to Dance) - Porter

"Largo" (Xerxes) - Haendel

"Liebestraum" (Dream of Love) - Liszt

"Londonderry Air" (Irish Folk Song)

"Long Ago and Far Away" (Cover Girl) - Kern

"Long, Long Ago" - Bayle

"Look for the Silver Lining" - Kern

"Lullaby" - Brahms

"Luxembourg Waltz" - Lehar

"Make Believe" (Showboat) - Kern

"Meditation" (Thais) - Massenet

"Melody in F" - Rubinstein

"Merry Widow Waltz" - Lehar

"My Old Kentucky Home" - Foster

"My Wild Irish Rose" - Olcott

"Night and Day" - Porter

"None but the Lonely Heart" - Tchaikowsky

"Oh Come All Ye Faithful" - Reading

"Old Folks at Home" - Foster

"Old Man River" (Showboat) - Kern

"The Old Refrain" - Kreisler

"On Wings of Song" - Mendelsohn

"O Promise Me" - Scott-DeKoven

"Over the Rainbow" - Harburg-Arlen

"La Paloma" - Yradier

"Revery" (Træumerei) - Schumann

"Romance" - Rubinstein

"Serenade" - Schubert

"Siboney" - Lecuona

"Silent Night" - Gruber

"Skater's Waltz" - Waldteufel

"Smoke Gets in Your Eyes (Roberta) - Kern

"Some Day" (Vagabond King) - Friml

"The Song is You" (Music in the Air) - Kern

"Song of India" (Sadko) - Rimsky-Korsakoff

"Song Without Words" - Tchaikowsky

"Song of Love" (Blossom Time) - Schubert-Romberg

"Spring Song" - Mendelsohn

"Stardust" - Carmichael

"Summertime" (Porgy and Bess) - Gershwin

"The Swan" - Saint-Sæns

"Swannee River" (American Folk Song)

"Swing Low Sweet Chariot" (Old Negro Spiritual)

"Tales from the Vienna Woods" (Waltz) - Johann Strauss

"Time on my Hands" (Smiles) - Youmans

"To a Wild Rose" (Woodland Sketches) - MacDowell

"Through the Years" - Youmans

"Vienna Blood" (Waltz) - Johann Strauss

"Waltz Dream" (Waltz) - Oscar Strauss

"Wanting You" (New Moon) - Romberg

"When Day is Done" - Katcher

"When I Grow Too Old to Dream" (The Night is Young) - Romberg

"When Irish Eyes are Smiling" - Olcott

"When You're Away" (The Only Girl) - Herbert

"Why Do I Love You" (Showboat) - Kern

JUDGING YOUR OWN WHISTLING TONES

Since your whistling tones, their quality, pitch, volume and rate of speed are largely governed by your ear, it follows that the significance of 'hearing yourself' as a guiding influence cannot be overestimated. The lack of ability to hear your own tones may be responsible for deficiencies in production. A bad whistling tone may be simply the result of inability to hear yourself or inability to know for what you are listening. You should be able to listen objectively and to criticize your own whistling. In order to assure rapid progress, you must maintain a high standard of self-criticism.

You cannot hear your own whistling tones exactly as others hear them. Therefore, it may be helpful to have a recording made from time to time. This will make it easier for you to analyze your whistling and to determine what needs to be corrected and improved.

If you have no recording facilities available, here is a way to hear yourself approximately as others hear you: Stand easily erect several inches from a corner of the room. Cup either one hand behind one ear or both hands behind both ears, pushing them very gently forward. Whistle directly into this corner. Try not to tense or to raise your shoulders. What you will hear is an approximation of how your whistling sounds to others.

The following self-tests are designed to aid you in

the evaluation of your own whistling. You will find that they will help you to discover and to overcome certain faults of which you were not even aware. These self-tests will serve further to summarize some of the things you have learned to do or to avoid.

All questions - to be answered by yes or no - are intended to point out specific shortcomings. The other segment lists groups of descriptive adjectives. Place check marks after those adjectives that best describe your whistling.

SELF-TESTS - BREATHING

Answer Yes or No

1. Is the posture of the body strained instead of well-balanced?

2. Does the body 'slump' instead of being easily erect?

3. Is the inhalation noisy instead of silent?

4. Is the inhalation forced instead of effortless?

5. Are the shoulders raised during the inhalation?

6. Is too much air inhaled, causing too great a pressure on the breathing apparatus?

7. Does some breath escape through the nose or mouth after the inhalation is completed and before you start to whistle?

8. Is the breath supply expelled too rapidly, resulting in a 'running out of breath' before a tone or a phrase is ended?

9. Does exaggerated pushing outward of the lower chest or pushing in and upward of the lower abdomen during exhalation prevent good breath management?

10. Do the tones lack good quality - fullness as well as steadiness - indicating inadequate management of breath?

11. Is the volume and carrying power of tone reduced because of improper management of breath?

12. Do you fail to renew your breath before you are conscious of being completely out of breath?

SELF-TESTS - QUALITY OF WHISTLING TONES

Place Check Marks Appropriately

Is the tone quality:

1. Weak, thin. . . . . Full, firm . . . .
2. Muffled. . . . . Clear . . . .
3. Flat, colorless. . . . . . . Well-rounded, rich. . . . . . .
4. Unsteady. . . . . Steady . . . .
5. Breathy . . . . Pure . . . .
6. Unpleasant . . . . Mellow. . . . .
7. Dull. . . . . Expressive. . . . .

Answer Yes or No

8. Is there a sort of clicking or grunting (K-like) sound at the start of the whistling tone?

9. Does some breath escape through the nose while you whistle?

10. Are the vibrato pulsations of the tone uneven or irregular in pitch extent?

11. Are the vibrato pulsations of the tone uneven or irregular in frequency or rapidity?

12. Are the low tones too dark in color?

13. Are the high tones shrill?

14. Is the tone produced with too obvious physical effort?

15. Do you fail to anticipate the desired quality or color immediately before you whistle a tone?

SELF-TESTS - THE LIPS, TONGUE, LOWER JAW AND SOFT PALATE

Answer Yes or No

1. Is there rigidity instead of a flexible, responsive condition in:
   A) The lips?
   B) The tongue?
   C) The lower jaw?
   D) The soft palate?

2. Are the lips pursed too tightly?

3. Are the lips too relaxed?

4. Do the center parts of the lips tend to touch each other while whistling?

5. Is the position of the lips changed unnecessarily?

6. Does the tongue seem to interfere with the flow of exhaled air to the lips?

7. Are the quivering motions of the tongue too slow?

8. Are the quivering motions of the tongue too fast?

9. Are the quivering motions of the tongue too weak?

10. Are the quivering motions of the tongue too strong?

11. Are the muscles of the lower jaw unduly tensed?

12. Does the soft palate raise too high?

13. Does the soft palate fail to raise at all?

14. Does a defective condition of the teeth or dentures impair the tones?

SELF-TESTS - PITCH

Answer Yes or No

1. Specifically, what causes you to whistle off key:

    A) Insufficient breath support (particularly when whistling very softly)?

    B) Excessive breath pressure in the lower chest and abdominal region during exhalation for whistling?

    C) Uneven vibrato pulsations of the tone?

    D) Whistling with too much volume (particularly the higher tones)?

    E) Lack of concentration upon the exact pitch of tone?

    F) Inability to hear yourself clearly?

    G) Mental and/or physical fatigue?

    H) Mental and/or physical tension?

2. Is there a tendency to whistle staccato tones off key?

3. Is there a tendency to flatten sustained tones, particularly the end of such tones?

4. Is there a tendency to flatten the end of phrases or passages?

5. Is there a tendency to flatten very slow phrases or passages?

6. Are the tones of ascending phrases and passages frequently sharpened?

7. Are the tones of descending phrases and passages frequently flattened?

SELF-TESTS - VOLUME

Answer Yes or No

1. When you increase the volume of whistling tones, are one or more of the following faults evident:

   A) Are the shoulders raised during the inhalation?

   B) Do the tones become unsteady?

   C) Does the tone quality change unfavorably?

   D) Does the tone volume tend to decrease markedly at the end of a phrase, indicating inadequate management of breath?

2. Are the tones generally too weak because of insufficient breath support?

3. Do you fail to anticipate the desired volume immediately before you whistle a tone?

4. Does the tone weaken immediately following the attack?

5. Is the beginning of a sustained tone or a phrase accented habitually?

6. Is the volume practically the same throughout the entire song instead of being varied?

7. Are sustained tones whistled without crescendo and/or decrescendo?

8. Are the crescendos and decrescendos, covering either one or more tones, whistled unevenly?

9. Are ascending phrases or passages whistled crescendo habitually?

10. Are descending phrases or passages whistled decrescendo habitually?

11. Is the tone volume inconsistent with the musical score and the meaning of the song?

12. Are there too frequent abrupt changes in volume?

13. Is the tone volume used unsuited to the size and the acoustical conditions of the room or hall?

14. Do you stand too close to one or more musical instruments or a record player while you whistle?

15. Is the accompaniment louder than your whistling?

SELF-TESTS - RATE OF SPEED

Answer Yes or No

1. Is the rate inconsistent with the musical score and with the meaning of the song?

2. Are some notes unduly prolonged?

3. Are the fast phrases or passages whistled too rapidly?

4. Do you fail to whistle legato tones smoothly and do you allow unnecessary breaks between succeeding legato tones?

5. Do you whistle staccato tones too hurriedly?

6. Are the staccato tones too loud or too penetrating?

7. Are there too frequent abrupt changes in the rate of speed within a song?

8. Is the rate of speed practically the same throughout the entire song instead of being varied?

9. Is the rate of speed slowed down habitually:

    A) When whistling very softly?

    B) When whistling a decrescendo?

    C) When whistling a descending phrase or passage?

10. Is the rate of speed accelerated habitually:

    A) When whistling with increased volume?

    B) When whistling a crescendo?

    C) When whistling an ascending phrase or passage?

11. Are the pauses between phrases and between passages too long or too short?

SELF-TESTS - GROUP WHISTLING

Answer Yes or No

In case you are the leader of a whistling group or choir:

1. Are you familiar with the outlined whistling techniques and with the fundamentals of music?

2. Do you assume a friendly and encouraging, as well as firm, attitude instead of being overly critical?

3. Do you plan practice or rehearsal sessions in advance?

4. While one division rehearses, are the other participants listening quietly and attentively?

5. Is the attack of tone simultaneous and precise?

6. Is the ending of phrases and passages simultaneous and precise?

7. Do all participants glide from one tone to the next following one at the same instant?

8. Do the participants try to memorize songs?

9. During rehearsal, are lighter songs alternated with more serious ones?

10. Do you avoid too prolonged practice sessions?

11. Do the participants seem to feel that group whistling is fun rather than a task?

CPSIA information can be obtained
at www.ICGtesting.com
Printed in the USA
BVHW061945270820
587362BV00005B/272